Let's Learn About
JAPAN
ACTIVITY & COLORING BOOK

Yuko Green

Did you know that Japanese children go to school for eleven months each year, or that Japan has special holidays just for boys and girls? Inside this exciting and educational coloring and activity book, you can learn all about the country of Japan while completing mazes, word searches, find-the-differences, and other fun activities. Find out what Japanese money is called, how to count to ten in Japanese, how to make animal sounds the same way that a Japanese child would, and much more.

Copyright
Copyright © 2013 by Yuko Green
All rights reserved.

Bibliographical Note
Let's Learn About JAPAN Activity and Coloring Book is a new work,
first published by Dover Publications in 2013.

International Standard Book Number
ISBN-13: 978-0-486-48993-3
ISBN-10: 0-486-48993-0

Manufactured in the United States by LSC Communications Book LLC
48993007   2021
www.doverpublications.com

JAPAN IN JAPANESE

日本

su

p

fis

m

g

on

et

How do you say JAPAN in Japanese? Japan translates to the "Land of the Rising Sun." To answer the question, fill in the missing letter to spell the name of each picture. The letters in the squares spell out the answer.

* Nihon (nee-hawn): another pronunciation is Nippon (ni-pon)

HOME SWEET HOME

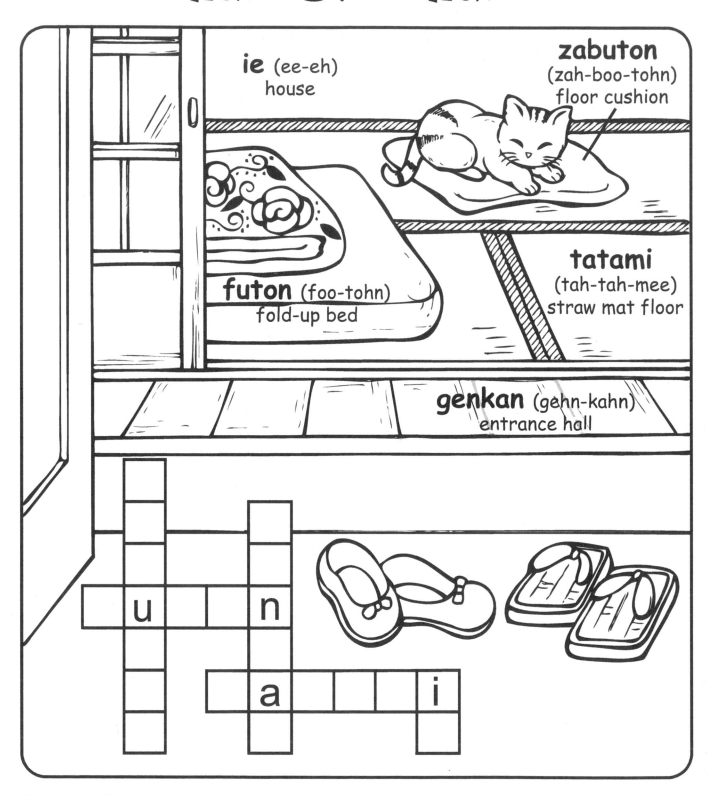

ie (ee-eh)
house

zabuton
(zah-boo-tohn)
floor cushion

futon (foo-tohn)
fold-up bed

tatami
(tah-tah-mee)
straw mat floor

genkan (gehn-kahn)
entrance hall

Did you know people in Japan take off their shoes at the doorway before going in the house, **ie** (ee-eh)? And that they sleep on the floor? Fill in the crossword with these names of things found in a Japanese house.

NUMBER MATCH-UPS
Japanese Toys

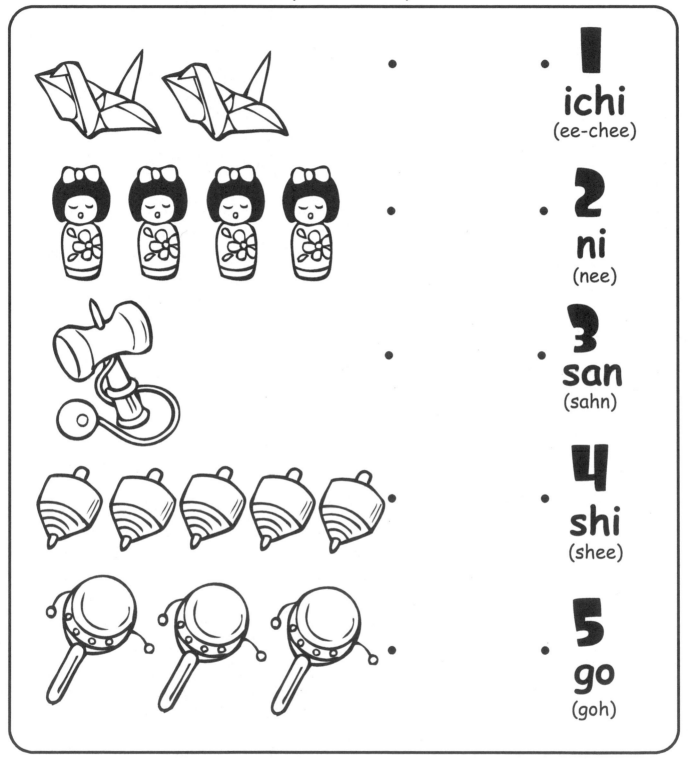

1 ichi (ee-chee)

2 ni (nee)

3 san (sahn)

4 shi (shee)

5 go (goh)

In each row, count the number of Japanese toys, and draw a line to the correct number on the right.
Learn how to say numbers in Japanese too.

POSTCARDS FROM JAPAN

○ = F
▲ = I
□ = J
★ = K
● = O
✿ = T
@ = U
☆ = Y

Hello from Japan's highest mountain,

Mt. _ _ _ _
     ○ @ □ ▲

Hi from Japan's capital city,

_ _ _ _ _
✿ ● ★ ☆ ●

Use the code to find out where the postcards are from.

4

MONEY MATH

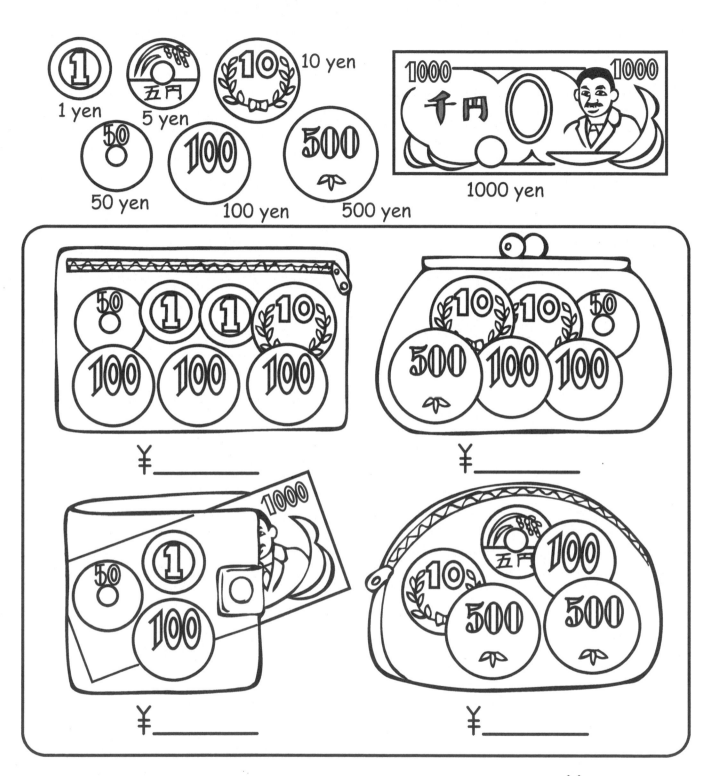

Japanese money is called yen. The symbol for yen is ¥.
Add up the money in each purse and write the amount on
the lines provided.

125 MILLION PEOPLE

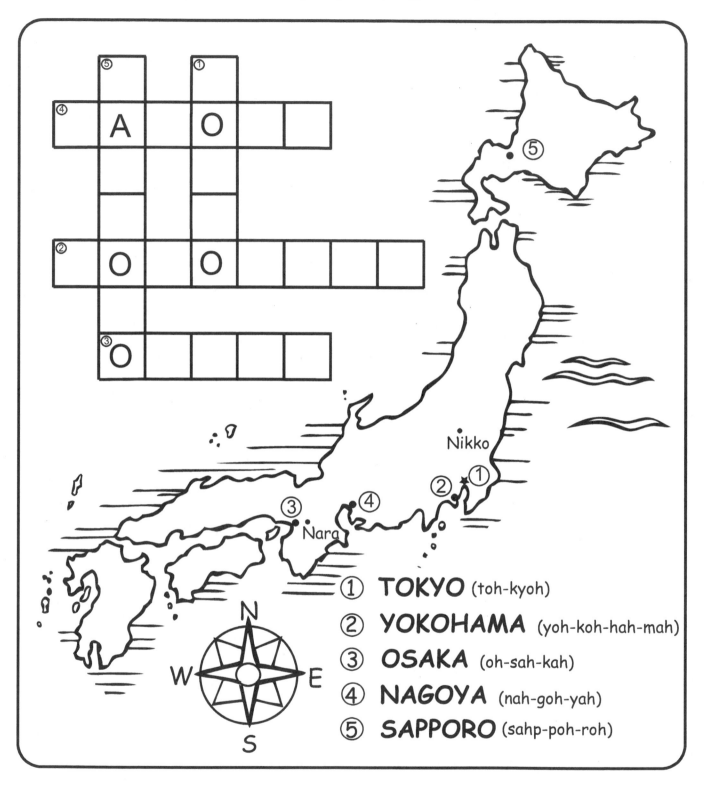

① **TOKYO** (toh-kyoh)

② **YOKOHAMA** (yoh-koh-hah-mah)

③ **OSAKA** (oh-sah-kah)

④ **NAGOYA** (nah-goh-yah)

⑤ **SAPPORO** (sahp-poh-roh)

Japan is made up of 4 major islands and over 3,000 small islands. Much of the country is mountainous, but most of the population lives in cities along the coastal plain and flat land.
Fill in the puzzle with the names of Japan's 5 major cities.

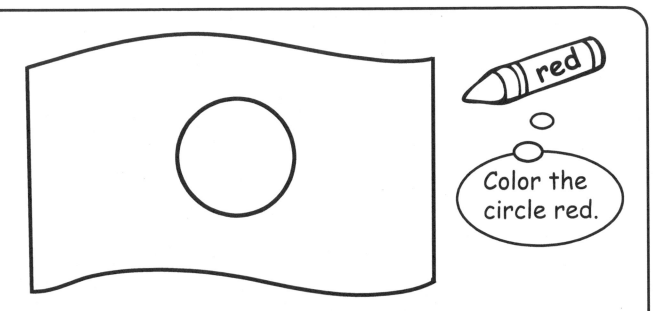

Color the circle red.

Find the opposite of each word, then use the numbered letters to complete the puzzle below.

left   _ _ _ _ _
         1

out   _ _
         2 4

fast   _ _ _ _
         3

small   _ _ _
             5

down   _ _
         6

The red circle in the Japanese flag symbolizes the

_ _ _ _ _ _   _ _ _
1 2 3 2 4 5   3 6 4

7

SPORTS IN JAPAN

r	k	u	a	n	d	o
u	y	k	e	k	j	m
k	s	a	l	u	u	s
e	u	r	k	f	d	a
d	m	a	s	y	o	u
n	o	t	o	p	u	r
o	k	e	n	d	o	k

yakyu
(yah-kyoo)

People in Japan enjoy many traditional sports as well as imported sports.

judo
(joo-doh)

karate
(kah-rah-teh)

kendo
(kehn-doh)

sumo
(soo-moh)

Find and circle each Japanese word for the different sports in the word search on the left page. Look across, down, and diagonally.

WHO AM I?
Japanese Animal Symbolism

とら **tora** (toh-rah) •
I run fast and am
a Japanese symbol
of power, passion, and
speed.

かめ **kame** (kah-meh) •
I move slowly and am
a symbol of long life.

つる **tsuru** (tsoo-roo) •
I am a Japanese
treasured bird and
am a symbol of happiness
and long life.

ちょう **chou** (choh) •
I fly with beautiful
wings and am a symbol
of joy.

Symbols are a large part of Japanese culture and are often used
in arts and crafts. Draw a line from the Japanese word to the
matching picture. Use the descriptions to help you.

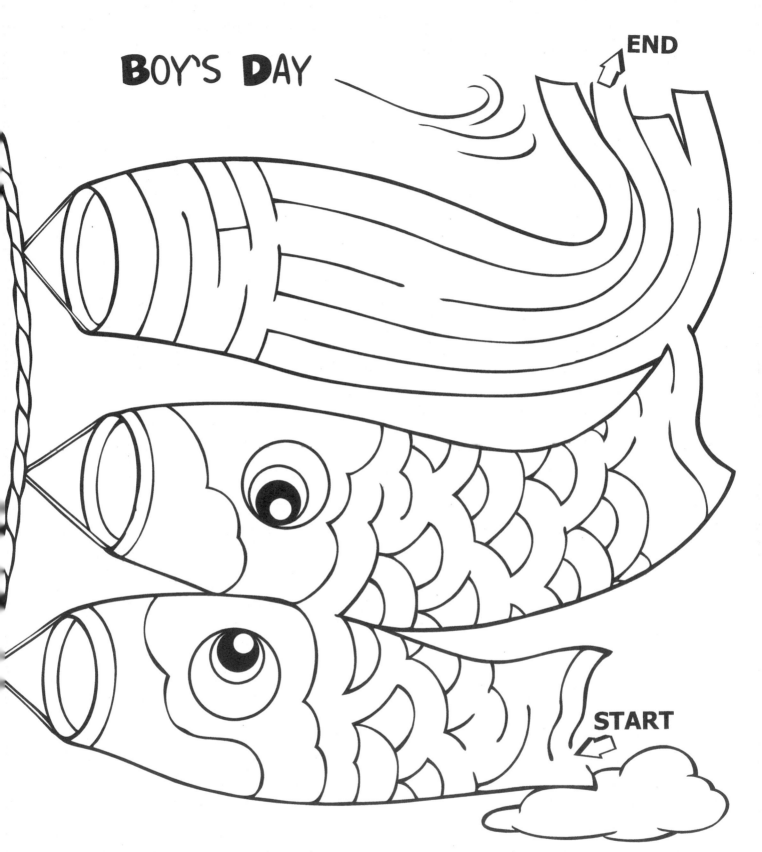

BOY'S DAY

END

START

May 5th is Boy's Day (also called Children's Day) in Japan.
Parents hang carp streamers high in the sky to celebrate the
healthy and strong growth of boys (children). Find a way to the
open sky through the carp maze.

BOY'S DAY ORIGAMI
PAPER-FOLDING ACTIVITY

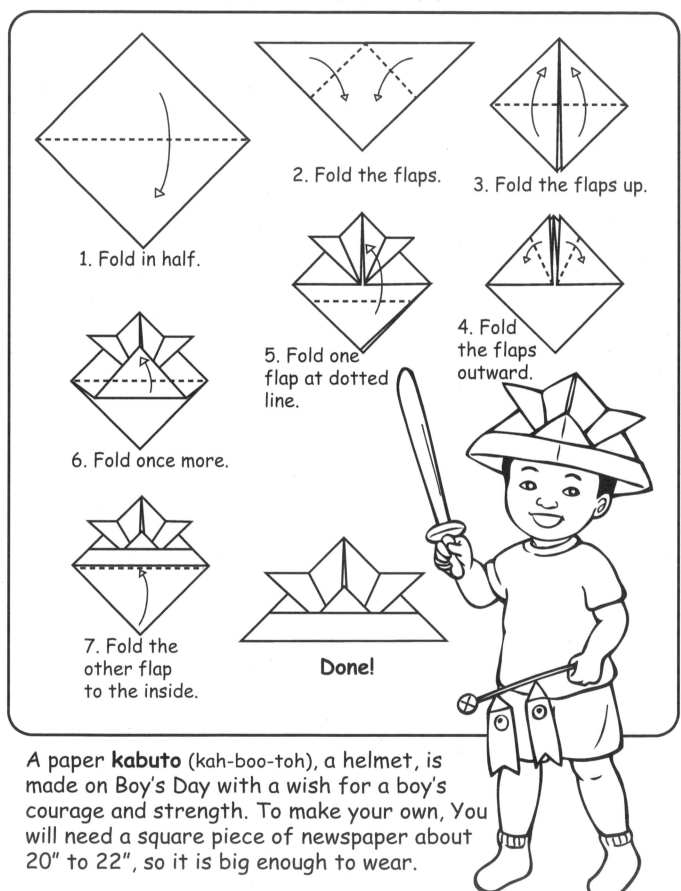

1. Fold in half.

2. Fold the flaps.

3. Fold the flaps up.

4. Fold the flaps outward.

5. Fold one flap at dotted line.

6. Fold once more.

7. Fold the other flap to the inside.

Done!

A paper **kabuto** (kah-boo-toh), a helmet, is made on Boy's Day with a wish for a boy's courage and strength. To make your own, You will need a square piece of newspaper about 20" to 22", so it is big enough to wear.

BOY'S DAY ORIGAMI
PAPER-FOLDING ACTIVITY

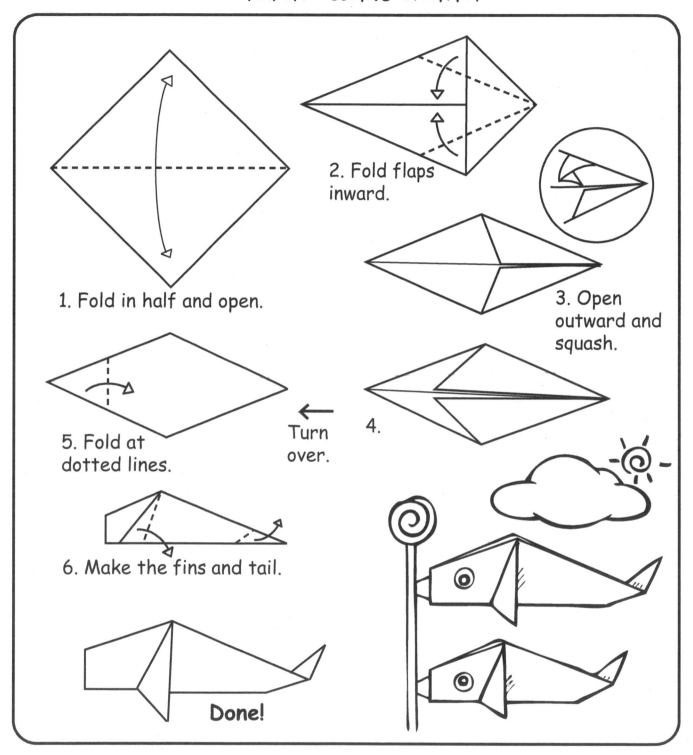

1. Fold in half and open.

2. Fold flaps inward.

3. Open outward and squash.

4.

Turn over.

5. Fold at dotted lines.

6. Make the fins and tail.

Done!

You can make origami carps in different sizes and colors. You will need: origami paper (standard 6" x 6" or any size), a chopstick (or any stick), glue, drawing paper, markers or crayons.
Draw a background and glue a chopstick to the carp. Have fun!

HIGH-TECH JAPAN

Japan is the world of technology. Find and circle the two toys that are exactly the same.

FOOD FUN WORD SEARCH

```
d f f s h b f f s
t e m p u r a y m
s q o b o s d u i
m o i c t i h b s
t o f u h w h i o
s u k i y a k i n
```

sushi
(soo-shee)

tempura
(tem-poo-rah)

sukiyaki
(soo-kee-yah-kee)

miso (soup)
(mee-soh)

tofu
(toh-foo)

(o) cha
(oh-chah)

Find and circle the bold words for Japanese food in the puzzle.
Look down, across, and diagonally.

DRESS-UP KIMONO

For boys: Popular Designs   For girls:

Most Japanese now wear Western-style clothes, but **kimonos** (kee-moh-nohs) are still worn on formal occasions and at festivals. Design and color the kimono for the girl above and the **yukata** (yuu-kah-tah), a light weight summer kimono, for the boy.

NUMBER MATCH-UPS
Gifts from Japan

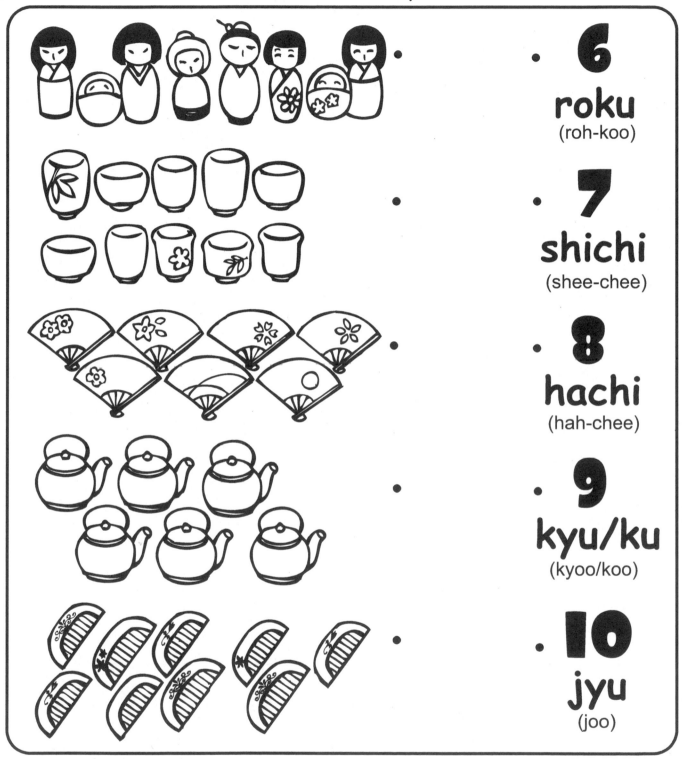

6
roku
(roh-koo)

7
shichi
(shee-chee)

8
hachi
(hah-chee)

9
kyu/ku
(kyoo/koo)

10
jyu
(joo)

Count each group of the Japanese items/souvenirs and draw a line to the correct number. Learn how to say the numbers in Japanese too.

SYMBOL SOLUTION

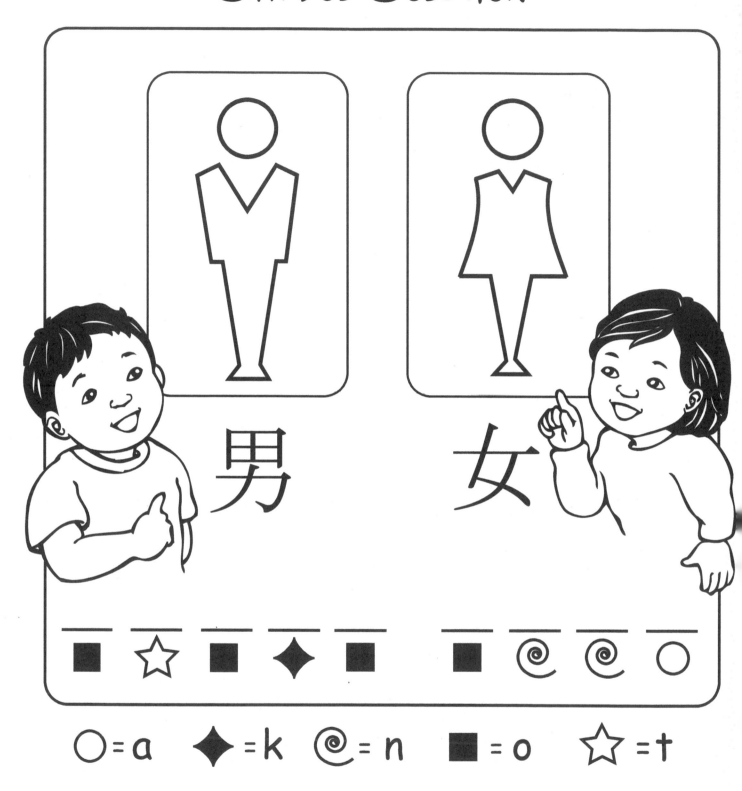

○ = a ◆ = k ◎ = n ■ = o ☆ = t

Use the shape code to read the Japanese symbols for man and woman. Write the letters in the blanks to find out how to say them.

* otoko (oh-toh-koh), onna (on-nah)

HIGH SPEED RIDE

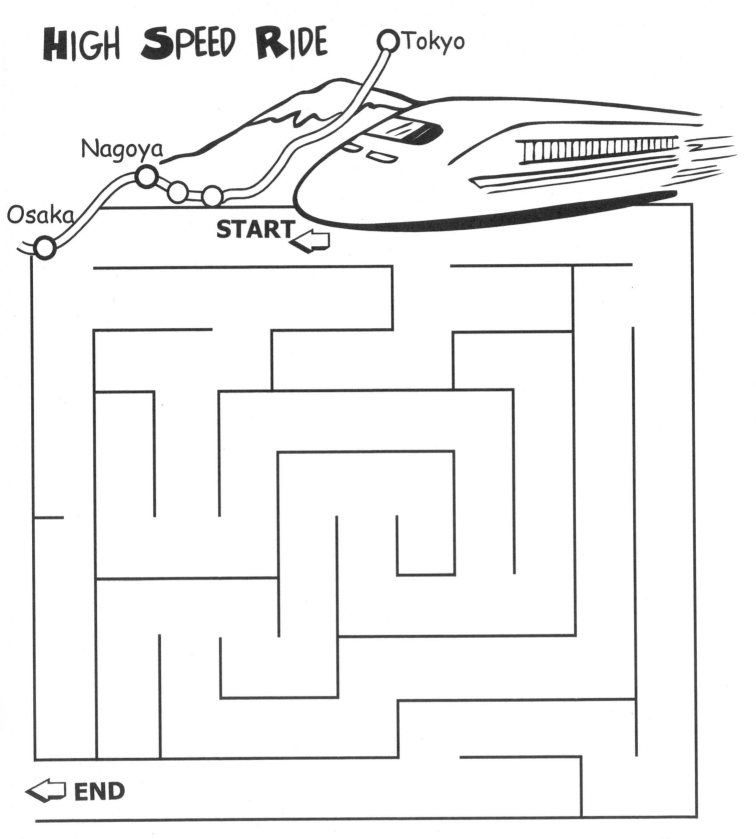

Tokyo

Nagoya

Osaka

START

END

Shinkansen (sheen-kan-sen) are Japan's high speed trains ("bullet trains"), running at speeds of up to 300 km/h (186 mph), connecting Japan's major cities. Take the above shinkansen through the maze as fast as you can!

VENDING MACHINE MATH

¥180

¥120

¥150

¥260

¥300

There are vending machines everywhere in Japan. You can buy drinks, snacks, toys, magazines, cell phones, games, food ... even eggs! Draw a line from each item to the group of coins you would need to buy it.

KOI MATCH

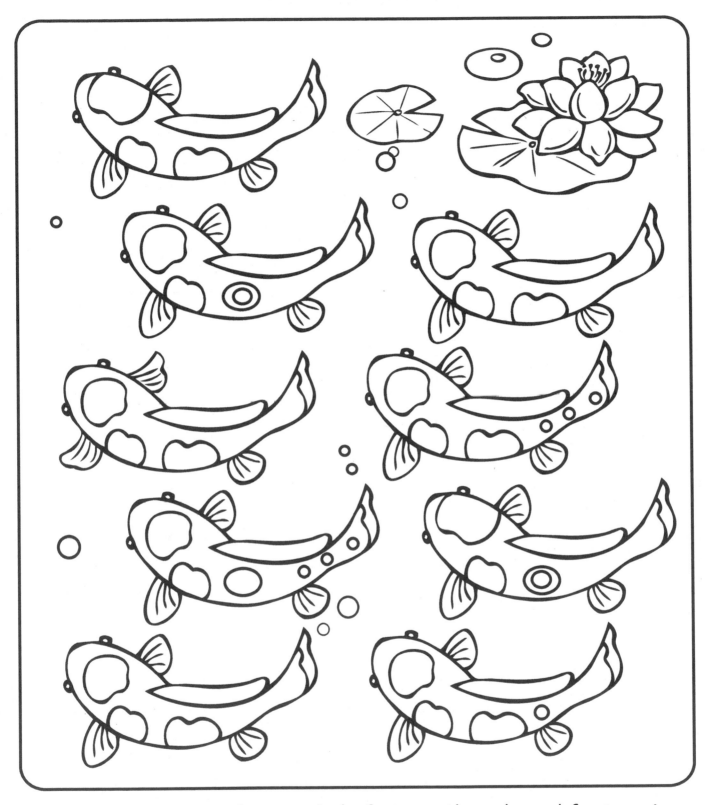

Koi (koh-ee), a carp, is a symbol of strength and good fortune in Japan. People keep these decorative fish as pets.
Find and circle the two koi that are exactly alike.

KYOTO MAZE

START

END

The city of **Kyoto** (kyoo-toh) is filled with temples, shrines and castles. Follow the rickshaw to explore nature and the seasons of Kyoto and to get to the Pagoda at the end.

SUMO WRESTLING

Sumo (suu-moh) is Japan's oldest sport, over 1,500 years old! Find and circle 10 things in the top picture that are different from the bottom picture.

HAPPY NEW YEAR!

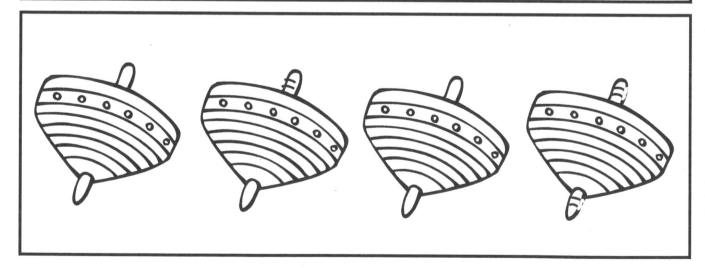

In each row of Japanese New Year's toys, find and circle the two pictures that look exactly the same.

KITE MAZE

Uh-oh, it's a kite traffic jam in the sky! Help the boy find his kite by following the string.

SCHOOL CHILDREN

- School, **gakko** (gahk-koh) starts in April and ends in March in Japan. Elementary school is from

  _____ grade to _____ grade.
  <u>first</u>   <u>sixth</u>

- Students have many fun activities like field trips to and historical places.

  _____ , _____
  <u>mountains</u>   <u>rivers</u>

- They walk to school every _____.
  <u>day</u>

- Students take their shoes off to keep the school clean. They mop _____ and _____ the
  <u>up</u>   <u>down</u>

  classroom floor every day after school.

一	六	日
first/one	six	day

山	川	上	下
mountain	river	up	down

Japanese children learn about 1000 basic kanji (Chinese characters) in elementary school! Draw the kanji characters in the blanks in the story above about school children.

GIRL'S DAY

Find and circle another princess doll exactly like me in the picture below.

March 3rd is **hina-matsuri** (hee-nah-mah-tsu-ree), Girl's Day, in Japan. Families display special dolls to celebrate and assure their daughter's healthy growth and happiness.

Nara Deer

Nara (nah-rah) is an ancient city, and a symbol of peace. Over 1000 tame deer roam Nara Park. Find and circle 10 things in the top picture that make it different from the bottom picture.

28

WHO AM I?
Foreign Words in Japan

テレビ **terebi** (teh-reh-bee) •
Watch me!

コーヒー **kohi** (koh-hee) •
Add milk and sugar to me
for a breakfast drink.

チョコ **choco** (cho-koh) •
I am a sweet treat.

トランプ **toranpu** (toh-run-poo) •
Play a game with me.

パン **pan** (pahn) •
Toast me for breakfast.

Many foreign words are used in Japan and written in katakana
characters. These words sound a little different in Japanese
from the original words. Draw a line from the Japanese word
of foreign origin on the left to the matching picture.

ANIMAL SOUNDS

```
m e e m e e o u g
y b x p y n n e a
m a o t e n l m a
k e r o k e r o g
p n c w b u p f a
k b e m v o m e a
n y a n y a o a e
w a n w a n q k v
```

gaa gaa
(gah-gah)

kero
kero
(keh-roh-
keh-roh)

How do you describe animal sounds in Japanese? Find and circle the animal sound words (bold) in the puzzle.
Look across, down, and diagonally.

SHIRO
Japanese Castle

START ➡

END ⬆

Japanese castles, **shiro** (shee-roh) were built for defense in warfare and as the homes of lords. The interior of the shiro was built in a confusing maze of paths leading to the castle keep. Find the way to the castle keep where the lord is hiding.

NIKKO MONKEYS

Find and circle 10 things in the top picture that make it different from the bottom picture of a carving of the three wise monkeys over the famous shrine in Nikko.

33

COLORS IN JAPAN

aka (red)
orenji (orange)
kiiro (yellow)
midori (green)
ao (blue)
murasaki (purple)
pinku (pink)

n o k i i r o m
m u r a s a k i
g o w e a y t d
g o p i n k u o
c y a j a j a r
k w x e o y i i

There are many beautiful gardens in Japan. Find and circle the 7 words for Japanese colors in the word search above. Look down, across, and diagonally. Pronunciation: aka (ah-kah), orenji (oh-rehn-jee), kiiro (kee-roh), midori (mee-doh-ree), ao (ah-oh), murasaki (moo-rah-sah-kee), pinku (peen-koo).

GREETING COMICS

1. Hello.   2. Good-bye.   3. Good morning.
4. Thank you.   5. I am sorry.   6. See you later.

Using the pictures as clues, guess what each comic is saying, and write the number of the correct answer on the lines provided.

LUCKY LAUGH

Fuku-warai (foo-koo-wah-rah-ee) is a face game that
Japanese children play around the New Year celebration.
The game is similar to that of Pin the Tail on the Donkey.

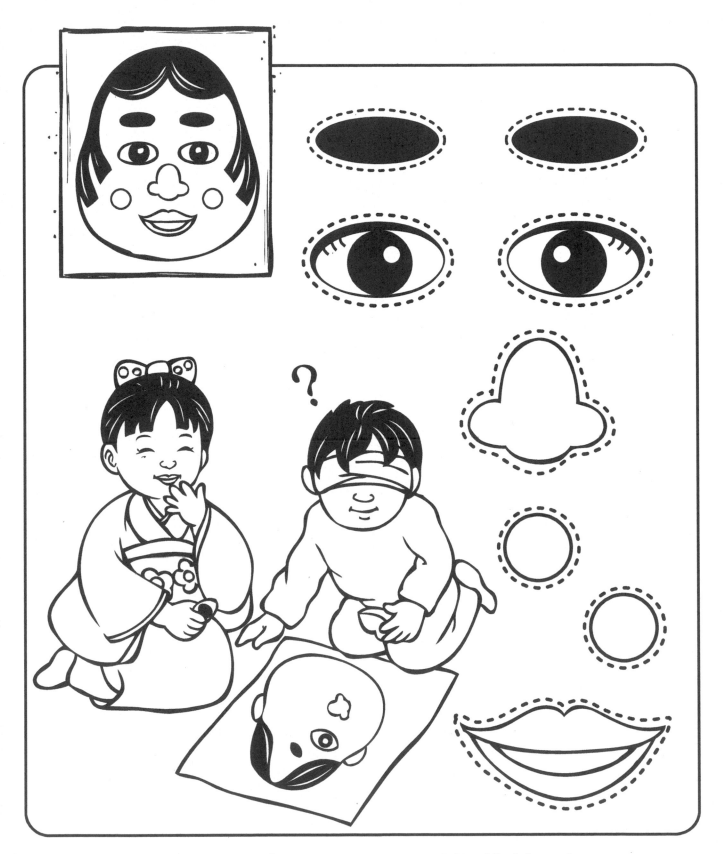

Cut out the parts on this page. Wear a blindfold and use tape to attach the pieces, and make a funny face. Your friend can hand you the parts and direct you, too.

SOLUTIONS

JAPAN IN JAPANESE

page 1

HOME SWEET HOME

page 2

NUMBER MATCH-UPS

Japanese Toys

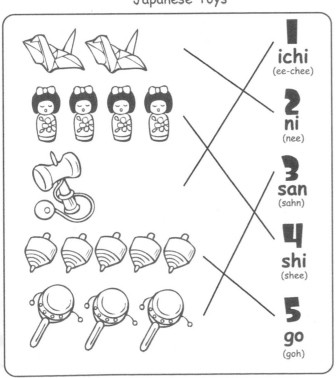

page 3

POSTCARDS FROM JAPAN

page 4

MONEY MATH

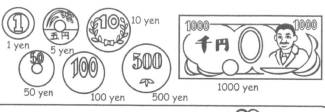

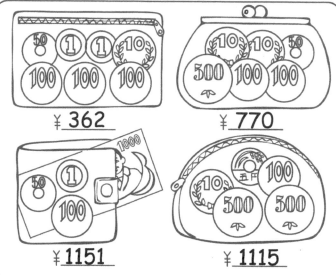

¥ 362   ¥ 770

¥ 1151   ¥ 1115

page 5

125 MILLION PEOPLE

```
  ⑤S        ①T
④N A G O Y A
  P        K
  P        Y
②Y O K O H A M A
  R
  ③O S A K A
```

① **TOKYO** (toh-kyoh)
② **YOKOHAMA** (yoh-kah-hah-mah)
③ **OSAKA** (oh-sah-kah)
④ **NAGOYA** (nah-goh-yah)
⑤ **SAPPORO** (sahp-poh-roh)

page 6

JAPAN'S FLAG

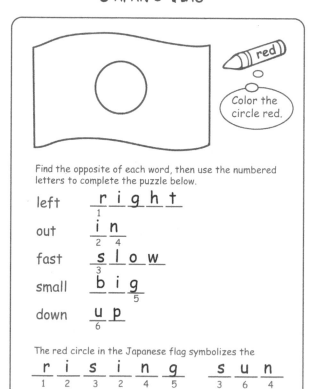

Color the circle red.

Find the opposite of each word, then use the numbered letters to complete the puzzle below.

left   r i g h t
       1

out   i n
     2 4

fast   s l o w
     3

small   b i g
        5

down   u p
      6

The red circle in the Japanese flag symbolizes the

r i s i n g   s u n
1 2 3 2 4 5   3 6 4

page 7

SPORTS IN JAPAN

```
R K U A N D O
U K E K U J O M
K S A E U D S A
E U A K F O U U
D R M S O P R R
N A T T P U O K
O K E N D O O K
```

yakyu
(yah-kyoo)

page 8

40

WHO AM I?
Japanese Animal Symbolism

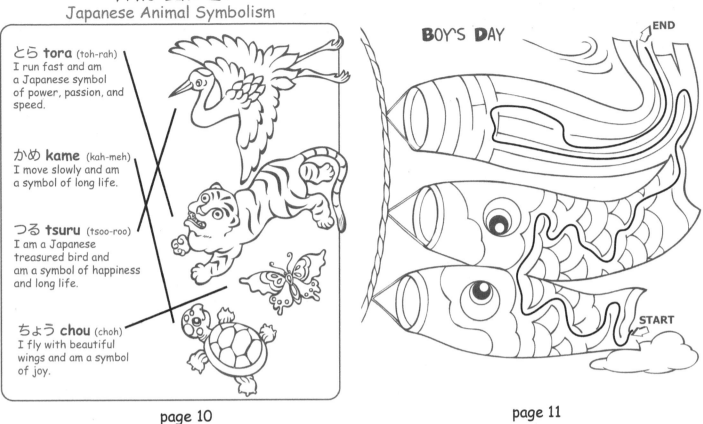

とら **tora** (toh-rah)
I run fast and am a Japanese symbol of power, passion, and speed.

かめ **kame** (kah-meh)
I move slowly and am a symbol of long life.

つる **tsuru** (tsoo-roo)
I am a Japanese treasured bird and am a symbol of happiness and long life.

ちょう **chou** (choh)
I fly with beautiful wings and am a symbol of joy.

page 10

BOY'S DAY

END

START

page 11

HIGH-TECH JAPAN

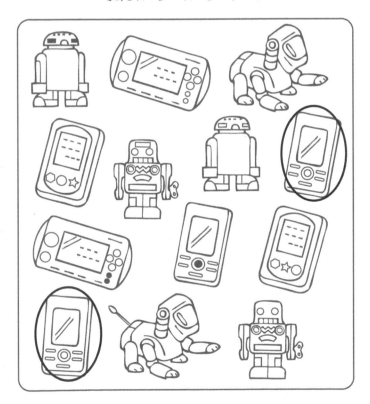

page 14

FOOD FUN WORD SEARCH

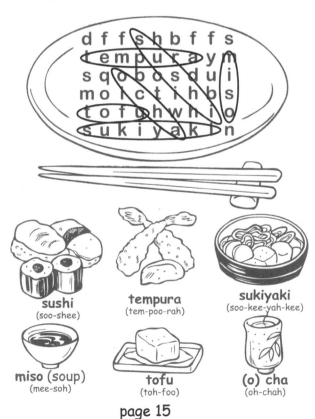

d f f s h b f f s
t e m p u r a y m
s q o o o s d u i
m o l c t i h b s
t o f u h w h i o
s u k i y a k i n

sushi
(soo-shee)

tempura
(tem-poo-rah)

sukiyaki
(soo-kee-yah-kee)

miso (soup)
(mee-soh)

tofu
(toh-foo)

(o) cha
(oh-chah)

page 15

NUMBER MATCH-UPS
Gifts from Japan

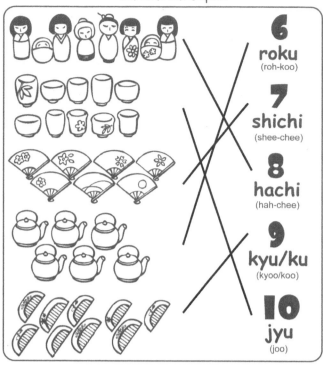

6
roku
(roh-koo)

7
shichi
(shee-chee)

8
hachi
(hah-chee)

9
kyu/ku
(kyoo/koo)

10
jyu
(joo)

page 17

SYMBOL SOLUTION

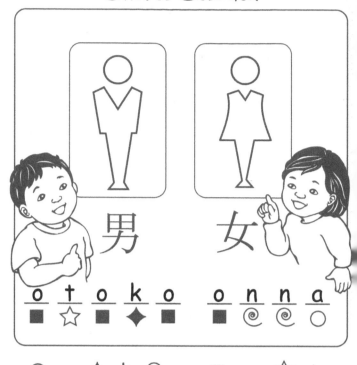

男　女

o t o k o　o n n a
■ ☆ ■ ◆ ■　■ ◎ ◎ ○

○ = a　◆ = k　◎ = n　■ = o　☆ = t

page 18

HIGH SPEED RIDE

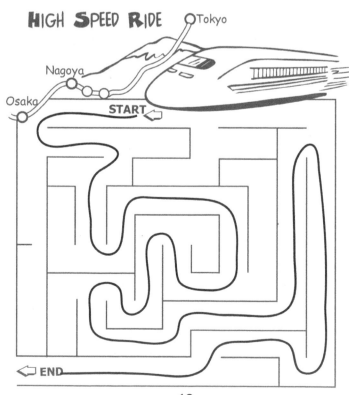

Tokyo

Nagoya

Osaka

START

END

page 19

VENDING MACHINE MATH

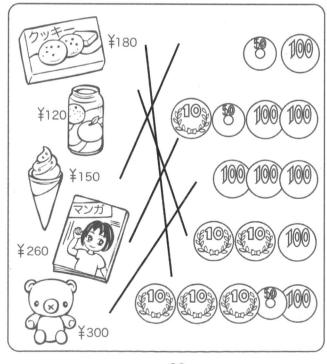

クッキー　¥180

¥120

¥150

マンガ

¥260

¥300

page 20

KOI MATCH

page 21

KYOTO MAZE

page 22

SUMO WRESTLING

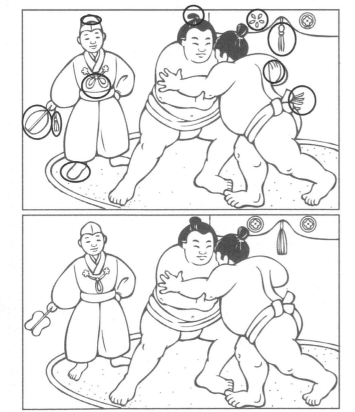

page 23

HAPPY NEW YEAR!

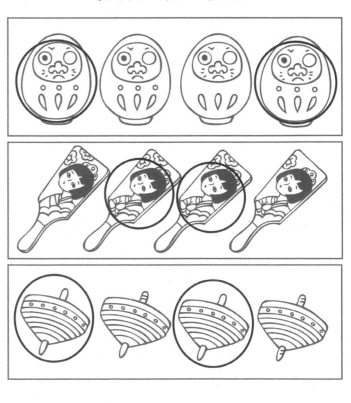

page 24

KITE MAZE

Uh-oh, it's a kite traffic jam in the sky! Help the boy find his kite and circle the number.

page 25

SCHOOL CHILDREN

- School, **gakko** (gahk-koh) starts in April and ends in March in Japan. Elementary school is from ___ (first) grade to 六 (sixth) grade.

- Students have many fun activities like field trips to 山 (mountains), 川 (rivers) and historical places.

- They walk to school every 日 (day).

- Students take their shoes off to keep the school clean. They mop 上 (up) and 下 (down) the classroom floor every day after school.

一 六 日
first/one   six   day

山 川 上 下
mountain river up down

page 26

GIRL'S DAY

Find and circle another princess doll exactly like me in the picture below.

page 27

NARA DEER

page 28

WHO AM I?
Foreign Words in Japan

テレビ **terebi** (teh-reh-bee)
Watch me!

コーヒー **kohi** (koh-hee)
Add milk and sugar to me
for a breakfast drink.

チョコ **choco** (cho-koh)
I am a sweet treat.

トランプ **toranpu** (toh-run-poo)
Play a game with me.

パン **pan** (pahn)
Toast me for breakfast.

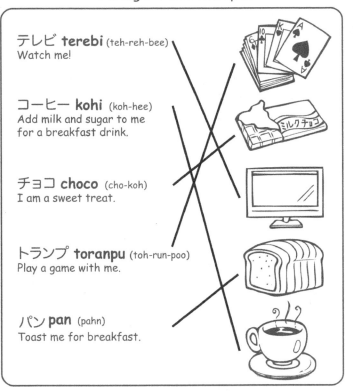

page 29

ANIMAL SOUNDS

page 30

SHIRO
Japanese Castle

page 32

NIKKO MONKEYS

page 33

COLORS IN JAPAN

aka (red)
orenji (orange)
kiiro (yellow)
midori (green)
ao (blue)
murasaki (purple)
pinku (pink)

```
n o k i i r o m
m u r a s a k i
g o w e a y t d
g o p i n k u o
c y a j a j a r
k w x e o y l i
```

page 34

GREETING COMICS

Ohayou.
(Oh-hah-yoh.)
3

Konnichiwa.
(Kohn-nee-chee-wah.)
1

Arigatou.
(Ah-ree-gah-toh.)
4

Gomennasai!
(Goh-men-nah-sai!)
5

Sayonara.
(Sah-yoh-nah-rah.)
2

Dewa mata.
(Day-wah ma-tah.)
6

1. Hello. 2. Good-bye. 3. Good morning.
4. Thank you. 5. I am sorry. 6. See you later.

page 35